DOUGHERTY
COUNTY
PUBLIC
LIBRARY

Harry Houdini

History Maker Bios

Janet Piehl

LERNER PUBLICATIONS COMPANY • MINNEAPOLIS

For L.W.

Illustrations by Tad Butler

Text copyright © 2009 by Janet Piehl
Illustrations copyright © 2009 by Lerner Publishing Group, Inc.

Lerner Publications Company
A division of Lerner Publishing Group, Inc.
241 First Avenue North
Minneapolis, MN 55401 U.S.A.

Website address: www.lernerbooks.com

Library of Congress Cataloging-in-Publication Data

Piehl, Janet.
    Harry Houdini / by Janet Piehl.
        p.   cm. — (History maker biographies)
    Includes bibliographical references and index.
    ISBN: 978–1–58013–705–8 (lib. bdg. : alk. paper)
        1. Houdini, Harry, 1874–1926—Juvenile literature. 2. Magicians—United
States—Biography—Juvenile literature. 3. Escape artists—United States—
Biography—Juvenile literature. I. Title.
GV1545.H8P54 2009
793.8092—dc22   2008025153

Manufactured in the United States of America
1 2 3 4 5 6 – PA – 14 13 12 11 10 09

TABLE OF CONTENTS

INTRODUCTION

The "World's Greatest Mystifier and King of Handcuffs." "The Greatest Mystery Show the World Has Ever Known." "Nothing on Earth Can Hold Houdini a Prisoner." These were just a few descriptions of Harry Houdini and his astounding shows. Harry could escape from jail cells and sealed water tanks. He could get out of nearly any pair of handcuffs. He could even make an elephant disappear.

But Harry was very poor as a boy. From childhood, he always worked hard to support his family. He also loved to amaze and entertain others. Harry performed in the late 1800s and early 1900s. He became the most famous magician and escape artist in history.

This is his story.

PRINCE OF THE AIR

The boy who grew up to be Harry Houdini was born on March 24, 1874. His name then was Erik Weisz. He and his family lived in Budapest, Hungary. Erik's father, Mayer Samuel Weisz, left for the United States when Erik was very young. Mayer Samuel settled in Appleton, Wisconsin. He worked as a rabbi, a Jewish religious leader.

In 1878, Erik and the rest of the family joined Mayer Samuel. The family's last name was changed to Weiss when they arrived in the United States. The spelling of Erik's name changed to Ehrich. Sometimes his family called him Ehrie.

Small-town Appleton was a good place for young children. Ehrich and his brothers could play in the parks. A traveling circus even passed through town. But Mayer Samuel had a hard time in Appleton. He lost his job. He moved his family to Milwaukee in 1882 to search for work.

The Weiss family moved to Milwaukee, Wisconsin (BELOW), a much larger city than Appleton. The family spoke mostly German at home.

Ehrich (shown here at the age of eight) and his brothers worked to help earn money for the family.

Mayer Samuel and his wife, Cecilia, had seven children to feed. The family was very poor. Instead of going to school, Ehrich and his brothers had to work much of the time. Ehrich sold newspapers and flowers. He shined shoes. Life was tough.

Ehrich once earned a few cents by putting on a circus with his friends. He remembered the circus he had seen in Appleton. Ehrich wore red woolen stockings, like real circus performers, and he swung from ropes. He tumbled and twisted his body. He called himself "Ehrich, the Prince of the Air."

In spite of Ehrich's help, the family was still poor. Twelve-year-old Ehrich decided it would be better for his family if he ran away. He hopped a train. He wanted to go to Texas. But there was a mix-up, and the train took him to Missouri instead. Ehrich found his way back to Wisconsin. Soon Mayer Samuel set off for New York City to find a new job. Ehrich joined him there.

By 1888, Ehrich's whole family was living in New York City. Mayer Samuel had found work. But they never had enough money. Ehrich still had to work. He took a job at a company that made neckties.

The necktie company where Ehrich worked might have looked like this tie workshop in New York City, pictured around 1889.

In his spare time, Ehrich ran, boxed, and swam. He enjoyed sports. He also liked learning about magic. He learned as much as he could about it. He read about a French magician named Jean Eugène Robert-Houdin. Jean Eugène's magic shows were amazing. He made orange trees blossom and grow. He made any drink pour out of bottles. Ehrich was fascinated.

KEY TO THE FUTURE

Many stories have been told about Ehrich's life. One story says that Ehrich once worked in a locksmith's shop. Locksmiths make and fix locks. One day, the locksmith left a hard task for Ehrich. The sheriff had brought in a man stuck in a pair of handcuffs. The key had broken off in the lock. Ehrich picked the lock with a piece of wire. The man was free. The locksmith was impressed with Ehrich's work. And Ehrich had found his future career.

Jean Eugène Robert-Houdin was a famous magician who died three years before Harry was born.

When he was seventeen, Ehrich teamed up with a friend named Jacob Hyman to do magic tricks. Jacob worked with Ehrich at the necktie company. Ehrich thought they should put on a magic show together. He took on a special stage name. Ehrich chose the last name Houdini, after Jean Eugène Robert-Houdin. He chose the first name Harry because it sounded like his nickname, Ehrie. Harry and Jacob called their magic act the Brothers Houdini.

In 1892, Harry's father became very ill. Mayer Samuel knew that he was dying. He asked Harry to promise to take care of his mother. Soon after, Mayer Samuel passed away.

2 THE HOUDINIS

Harry needed to make a living. He remembered his promise to his father. He decided to support his mother by performing magic shows. This time, he worked with his brother Theo. The brothers did tricks with cards. They charmed snakes. They made mango trees appear out of nowhere. Harry earned a little pay. He gave his extra money to his mother.

Harry kept his act's name. He and Theo (LEFT) called themselves the Brothers Houdini.

The brothers' most amazing trick was called the Metamorphosis. Harry and Theo stood onstage with a large trunk. Harry was tied up and put into a cloth sack. Then he was locked inside the trunk. Theo pulled a curtain in front of himself and the trunk. He clapped three times. Then the curtain opened. There was Harry, free from the rope, sack, and trunk! Next, Harry opened the trunk. Theo was inside! The quick escape and switch mystified audiences.

The brothers' act was becoming popular. But soon, Harry met a singer and dancer named Wilhelmina Beatrice Rahner. She went by Bess for short. Harry and Bess fell in love. They married in the summer of 1894. Bess replaced Theo as Harry's partner onstage.

Harry and his new wife Bess performed together as the Houdinis.

Popular circuses, like the circus shown in this poster, gave Harry and Bess ideas of what people liked to see.

Harry and Bess took their magic show on the road. The Houdinis played in dime museums all over the United States. Dime museums were theaters where many unusual acts performed. Harry and Bess also traveled with circuses. They worked with an armless man who played the violin with his toes, a needle swallower, strongmen, and acrobats. Harry tried to learn something from all of them.

Harry and Bess performed the Metamorphosis. Audiences were shocked to see Harry and Bess trade places in as little as three seconds. Harry started to experiment with handcuff escapes. He would go to a local police station and ask to be handcuffed. He could escape from most sets of handcuffs, sometimes in less than one minute. Later, onstage, Harry would be handcuffed in the Metamorphosis trunk. He could still complete the escape quickly. But no one seemed very interested in the handcuff escapes.

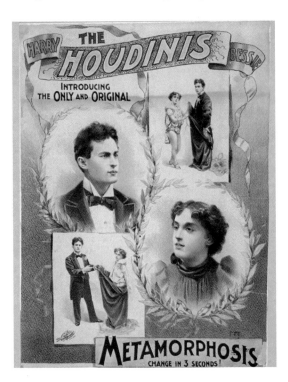

Audiences loved to see Harry and Bess trade places.

Harry performed many of his tricks behind a booth or frame with a curtain in the front. He called this his cabinet. This way, audiences couldn't see his escapes. It added a sense of mystery to Harry's act. The cabinet also prevented others from learning his tricks.

Harry and Bess also put on séances. Séances are meetings in which people try to talk to the dead. Harry and Bess pretended to be mediums. Mediums are people who believe that they can get in touch with dead people.

Audiences loved the séances. They came to hear messages from loved ones who had passed away. But Harry knew that he and Bess didn't really talk to dead people. Their messages were usually lucky guesses. He felt bad for giving people false hope of reaching dead loved ones. He and Bess stopped doing séances.

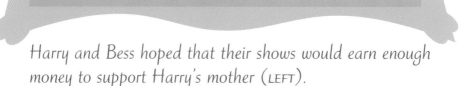

Harry and Bess hoped that their shows would earn enough money to support Harry's mother (LEFT).

Harry and Bess worked hard. But they earned little money. There wasn't much left over to give Harry's mother. Harry was ready to give up.

Things began to change in 1899. A man named Martin Beck saw one of the Houdinis' shows. Martin was a theater manager. He was impressed with Harry's handcuff escapes. He set up shows for the Houdinis in his theaters.

Harry continued to perform his handcuff escapes. They finally began to excite audiences. And Harry added a trick he'd learned in the dime museums. He swallowed as many as 150 needles. Then he put a long piece of thread down his throat. He tugged on the end of the thread. He pulled up the very same needles from his throat. The needles were threaded!

Harry's handcuff tricks became popular at last.

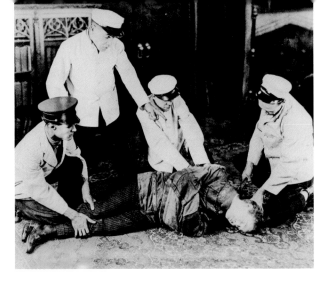

Harry performs his straitjacket escape during a show.

Another new trick Harry did was the straitjacket escape. Straitjackets are garments used to restrain violent prisoners or patients. They hold people's arms close to their bodies so they can't hurt themselves or others. The arms cross in front. The sleeves are sewn shut. Straitjackets buckle or lace shut in the back. Most people can't get out of a straitjacket. But Harry could, often in less than three minutes. Audiences loved the trick.

Finally, Harry and Bess were earning good wages. They had more than enough money to send to Harry's mother. In the spring of 1900, Harry and Bess felt successful enough to take their act to Europe.

3 KING OF HANDCUFFS

The Houdinis' first European stop was London. They performed at a large theater called the Alhambra. They introduced the Metamorphosis trick and Harry's handcuff escapes to excited crowds.

Harry bet his audiences that there was no lock he couldn't overcome.

Harry called himself the King of Handcuffs and the World's Greatest Mystifier. He challenged audiences to bring him handcuffs that he couldn't master. Most of the time, Harry freed himself quickly. But one night in Blackburn, England, Harry almost didn't escape. A bodybuilder named William Hodgson took Harry's challenge. He locked and chained Harry's arms and put two pairs of handcuffs on his wrists. William also chained and cuffed Harry's legs and ankles. Harry was barely able to move. But he went behind his cabinet to try to free himself.

After almost two hours, Harry emerged. His shirt was torn. His arms and wrists were swollen, gashed, and bleeding. He could hardly stand. But he was free! The audience cheered for fifteen minutes.

Harry and Bess performed in countries such as Germany, the Netherlands, Denmark, France, and Russia. They returned to the United States in the summer of 1905. Harry bought a house in New York City. The house was big enough for Harry's mother, Cecilia; his brother Leopold; and his sister, Gladys, to move in. Harry was proud to provide for his family.

This poster was for one of Harry's shows in Germany.

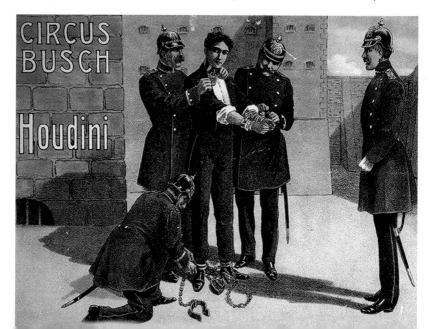

Harry and Bess started a new tour of the United States. Harry kept doing the handcuff escapes that had been so successful in Europe.

Harry also continued to visit police stations to show off his escape skills. He invited police officers and newspaper reporters to watch. He stripped off his clothes to show that he was not hiding any tools that could be used to pick a lock. Then the police locked him in a cell. Soon, Harry had escaped.

HOUDINI WHO?

Many magicians tried to copy Harry. They tried to perform escapes like his. They also used names that sounded like Harry Houdini. Harry's imitators included Hougini, Coutini, Kleppini, Harry Rudini, and Harry Mourdini.

Harry disliked his imitators. He tried to shut down many of their acts. But Harry approved of one copycat—his own brother Theo. Theo performed as Hardeen. He attracted copycats of his own. One of them called himself Hardini!

Harry jumps handcuffed into the Charles River in Boston.

The shocked reporters wrote about Harry's escapes in their newspapers. Harry loved the attention. It helped create interest in his shows.

Harry found a new, dangerous way to stir up interest in his shows. He stood on a bridge and allowed himself to be handcuffed. Then he jumped into the water. Nervous crowds of people watched. Soon, Harry's head bobbed up. He waved his hands. He was out of the handcuffs! The crowds cheered wildly.

Harry tried another death-defying feat for his stage shows. It was known as the Milk Can Escape. Stagehands filled a giant milk can with water. The milk can was large enough that a man could fit inside of it. Harry stepped into the can and crouched down inside it. Then an assistant shut and padlocked the can's lid. Another assistant stood by with an ax, ready to smash the can in case Harry didn't come out. But Harry did come out. He usually escaped in about two minutes. The audience was amazed to see the can's lid and locks still in place.

This poster shows Harry getting ready for his Milk Can Escape.

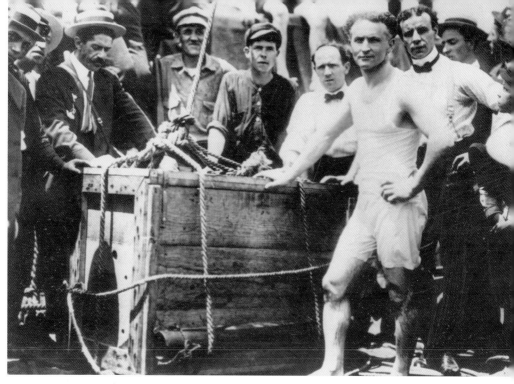

Harry (FRONT RIGHT) even escaped from a packing crate lowered into the icy Detroit River in 1907.

Harry performed his escapes all over the United States. He and Bess returned to Europe to show off his bridge jumps and Milk Can Escape there. By early 1910, Harry was ready to conquer a new continent: Australia.

4 Down Under and Upside Down

Harry wanted to take his escapes and magic to Australia. He also wanted to be the first person to fly an airplane in Australia. The Wright brothers had made the first flight in 1903, in North Carolina. Since then, airplanes had slowly caught on.

Early airplanes were dangerous. The weather had to be just right to fly. But Harry was no stranger to danger. He hoped to use airplanes in his stunts. So Harry bought a plane and learned to fly.

Harry and Bess made the long journey by ship to Australia. Harry staked out a field near Melbourne. He waited for the weather to be calm. Finally, on March 18, 1910, Harry took off. He flew for about one minute. He made several more flights that lasted up to four minutes. He climbed about one hundred feet off the ground. Harry had made the first flights in Australia.

The Aerial League of Australia gave Harry a trophy. He was the first to fly in that country.

Harry kept creating new tricks. In 1912, he introduced a stunt called the Water Torture Cell, or the Upside Down. Harry appeared onstage with a water tank with glass sides. Harry's feet were locked into a fixture on the lid of the tank. Harry was lowered headfirst into the full water tank. Then his assistants locked the tank shut. They pulled a curtain in front of the tank. They stood ready with axes in case the tank needed to be smashed open. Within two minutes, Harry had escaped! Surprisingly, the lid was still intact.

In the summer of 1913, Harry set out for another tour of Europe. He sadly bid good-bye to his mother. She had been feeling poorly. He worried that he might not see her again. In Copenhagen, Denmark, Harry got the news that Cecilia had died. He rushed home for her funeral.

The next few years were hard for Harry. He missed his mother terribly. She was never far from Harry's mind.

Still, Harry went on performing. He put a new twist on his straitjacket escape. In 1915, he escaped from a straitjacket while hanging by his ankles, forty-five feet off the ground.

Harry performs his straitjacket escape hanging over a subway building site in New York City.

Harry did his new straitjacket stunt in any city with tall buildings. Sometimes he hung nine or more stories above the ground. It usually took him three minutes or less to free himself. Huge crowds watched in awe. One hundred thousand people came to see him do this straitjacket escape in Washington, D.C., in 1916. People loved seeing Houdini risk death.

TRUTH OR FICTION?

Sometimes Harry made up details about his life. If something sounded good, he'd pretend it was true.

Harry was born in Budapest, Hungary. But he often told people he was born in Appleton. He wanted people to think he was born in the United States.

Harry posed for a group photo with President Theodore Roosevelt. He erased everyone from the photo except himself and Roosevelt. It looked as if the strangers were close friends.

Even when his life was not in danger, Harry thrilled audiences. At some of his shows, Harry made an elephant disappear. At New York City's Hippodrome, an eight-foot-tall elephant named Jennie joined Harry onstage. Behind him was a huge box with curtains. Harry sent Jennie into the box and shut its curtains. The curtains opened seconds later. Jennie was gone! The crowd was shocked. "Even the elephant doesn't know how it is done," said Harry.

Harry and Jennie appear at the Hippodrome in New York City.

Harry knew that his stunts worked well in the street and on the stage. He wanted to perform his feats in films too. In the early 1900s, silent movies were becoming popular. Harry made several movies. In his films, Harry battled a giant robot, survived a plane crash, worked as a secret government agent, and made countless escapes. The films were fairly popular.

But films weren't making Harry enough money. In 1923, he decided to go back to the stage.

5 SPIRITS AND STUNTS

Harry had become the world's most famous magician and one of the most popular entertainers. He enjoyed meeting other famous people. He became friends with Sir Arthur Conan Doyle, the Scottish author of the Sherlock Holmes mysteries. Sir Arthur's wife, Lady Jean, was a medium. She said that she could speak to spirits, or the dead.

Sir Arthur Conan Doyle (LEFT) and Harry in London

Harry remembered his own days as a medium. He knew that most mediums were fakes. But he was willing to believe that it was possible to contact the dead. Harry missed his mother. He held on to hope that he would speak to her again. Lady Jean held a séance with Harry. It seemed as if she had contacted Harry's mother. Lady Jean wrote pages of messages from Cecilia in English.

But Harry knew that his mother spoke German. She would not have contacted Harry in English. Lady Jean's séance was a fake. Harry's friendship with Lady Jean and Sir Arthur was never the same again.

Harry believed that fake mediums took advantage of people's sorrow. He began to investigate other mediums. He joined a committee that would give a prize to someone who could produce real evidence of spirits. The contest was sponsored by the magazine *Scientific American.*

They investigated a Boston medium named Mina Crandon. People called her Margery. Margery brought messages from the spirits through her dead brother, Walter. At her séances, yellow rosebuds grew on the table. The table rose off the floor. Objects moved by themselves. Many people believed that Margery was the real thing.

Many believed that Margery (CENTER) spoke with the dead.

Harry felt that Margery's contacts with the dead were fake. He tested her in many ways. He showed that Margery was producing the effects and moving the objects herself. In 1925, the committee voted not to give her the *Scientific American* prize.

Harry talked about mediums at his shows. Harry gave demonstrations of séances. He showed how fake mediums used magic and pretended that spirits produced the effects. Harry also published a book about fake mediums called *A Magician Among the Spirits.*

Harry tested Margery by making her hold a séance sitting inside a box. He wanted to prove that she was using her own body to move things.

SUPERNATURAL OR JUST SUPER?

Some people were convinced that Harry had supernatural powers, or powers that natural laws cannot explain. They thought his body could pass through solid objects. Sir Arthur Conan Doyle thought Harry was a real medium. Harry denied having such abilities.

But rumors about his supernatural powers may have increased interest in his shows and stunts.

Some people still claim that this clay bust of Harry is haunted.

Harry continued his magic tricks and stunts. He did the Metamorphosis, the needle-swallowing trick, and the Upside Down. He even survived for one hour and thirty-one minutes in a sealed coffin at the bottom of a swimming pool.

Harry prepares to perform an escape in a pool in 1926.

At the age of fifty-two, Harry worried that his days were numbered. His stunts were hard on his body. At a show in Albany, New York, in October 1926, he broke his left ankle doing the Upside Down. But Harry hated to miss shows. So he kept performing.

He went on to Montreal. There, he met with some students in his dressing room. One of them asked if it was true that punches to his stomach did not hurt Harry. The student asked if he could punch Harry. Harry accepted the challenge. Before Harry could prepare himself, the student violently punched him in the right side.

A few hours later, Harry was in great pain. Still, he would not stop his shows. He went on to Detroit. After his show that night, he was rushed to the hospital. He didn't want to go. But his doctors insisted he must.

Harry's appendix had burst. He also had a bad infection. Doctors tried to save him, but it was too late. Harry died on October 31, 1926.

Death Chains Ball Houdini in Battle To Break Shackles Of Grim Reaper

Student's Blow to Stomach Brought Fatal Illness, Physicians Declare

Special by Leased Wire to The Chronicle

DETROIT, Mich., Oct. 31.—Harry Houdini came Sunday to the one shackle he could not fathom in life. He died in Grace Hospital at 1:30 o'clock this afternoon after a week's illness. The cause of death was given as diffuse streptococca peritonitis, the result of a ruptured appendix.

As he had wished, the magician, one of the leading characters of the American stage, was stricken in the midst of things he loved best in the world.

He gave a performance at the Garrick Theater last Sunday evening in spite of a high temperature and a physician's warning, because he would not break faith with an audience which had packed the theater to watch his conjuring.

ILLNESS RESULT OF BLOW

Houdini's fatal illness was the result of a blow given him by a student at McGill University, Montreal, week before last, friends say.

Houdini had lectured before the student body and in the open forum which followed was questioned as to the possibility of needles as

that have remained in Detroit with Mrs. Houdini.

Funeral arrangements will not be arranged until their arrival in New York Tuesday morning.
(Copyright, 1926, Chicago Tribune Press Service)

HOUDINI WAS NOTABLE ON AMERICAN STAGE

DETROIT, Oct. 31 (AP)—As one of the outstanding personages of the American stage and leader of magicians, Harry Houdini's popularity lasted for a quarter century.

As one of the outstanding personages of the American stage and leader of magicians, his popularity lasted for a quarter century.

Houdini counted among his audiences the royalty of Europe and Asia. He wrote numerous treatises intended to expose spiritualism as a fraud. His book, "A Magician Among the Spirits," created a furore among professional spiritualists by its assertions that the practice was "bunk."

BEATS NOTABLE FEAT

One of his public challenges of long standing that he could duplicate or expose any seemingly magic feat was accepted by Ramon Bey, Egyptian mystifier, in August. The Egyptian had created a sensation by remaining in a sealed coffin under water for nineteen minutes. "Short breaths and conservation of oxygen," said Houdini, who entered the coffin and stayed there ninety minutes, "did it."

A handcuffed prisoner brought into Appleton, Wis., by a Sheriff who had lost the keys to the handcuffs was the occasion for the discovery of the trick of opening of handcuffs which Houdini said was known only to him, his wife and the prisoner.

ADEPT IN ESCAPES

Besides performing various so-called magical tricks, Houdini was adept in releasing himself from almost any kind of confinement that could be devised. He freed himself after being manacled and shut in a box. He freed himself hung from a derrick in midair and a strait-jacket. He freed himself to be confined under water. Although he challenged any man to confine him, no man ever escaped from any of them.

Houdini leaves his widow, who was Wilhelmina Rahner of Brooklyn. They were married in

Throughout his long career as professional magician Harry Houdini prided himself particularly on being a practical performer in his line. He wrapped himself in a cloak of mystery as had others of his kind and he laid no claim to the possession of peculiarly supernormal powers in carrying out his puzzling and illusive sleight-of-hand tricks. The mystery of his

> Newspapers across the United States announced Harry's death.

Harry's brother Theo and Bess visit Harry's grave.

Bess felt lost without Harry. She held
séances to try to contact him. She said he
had given her a code before he died. He
would give her the code if she succeeded in
contacting him. But Bess never got through
to Harry. Ten years after Harry died, on
Halloween 1936, she tried one last séance.
She heard nothing from Harry. At last, Bess
gave up.

Harry had escaped from many things. He could break out of handcuffs, straitjackets, giant milk cans, and the Water Torture Cell. But Harry could not escape death. He is buried next to his parents in Machpelah Cemetery in New York. Many people visit his grave every year. Harry is gone, but the magic of his memory lives on.

Each year, magicians visit Harry's grave to honor his remarkable life.

TIMELINE

In the year . . .

1878   Harry and his family joined his father in Appleton, Wisconsin.

1882   his family moved to Milwaukee, Wisconsin.

1888   his family lived in New York City.

1891   he began using the name Harry Houdini.   Age 17

1892   his father died on October 5.

1894   he married Bess Rahner on June 22.

1899   Martin Beck hired Harry and Bess to perform at his theaters.

1900   Harry and Bess toured Europe for the first time.   Age 26

1905   they returned to the United States and bought a house in New York City.

1907   Harry performed his first handcuffed bridge jump.

1908   he performed his first Milk Can Escape.

1910   he became the first person to successfully fly an airplane in Australia.

1912   he performed his first Upside Down stunt.   Age 38

1913   his mother died on July 17.

1915   he performed his first suspended straitjacket escape.

1919   his first movie was released.   Age 45

1920   he met Sir Arthur Conan Doyle.

1925   he exposed fake mediums such as Margery.

1926   he died on October 31 in Detroit, Michigan.   Age 52

HOW DID HE DO IT?

Like most magicians, Harry guarded his secrets carefully. Some of his methods may never be known. For example, no one knows exactly how the Upside Down worked. But some of Harry's secrets have been uncovered.

We know that Harry studied handcuffs carefully to learn how to escape from them. For his jail breaks, he sometimes hid a key in his hair or in a false sixth finger. Sometimes he secretly cut the laces of a straitjacket. In the Milk Can Escape, the can appeared securely shut to the audience. In fact, the neck of the can was not fixed to the rest of the can. The can could be opened only from inside. Harry's biggest secret was his genius at deception.

FURTHER READING

Ho, Oliver. *Young Magician: Magic Tricks.* **New York: Sterling Publishing, 2005.** This book has instructions on how to do twenty-three magic tricks.

Krull, Kathleen. *Houdini: World's Greatest Mystery Man and Escape King.* **New York: Walker and Company, 2005.** This picture-book biography tells Harry Houdini's life story and highlights some of his greatest feats.

Kulling, Monica. *The Great Houdini.* **New York: Random House, 1999.** A story version of Harry Houdini's life covers his most famous tricks.

MacLeod, Elizabeth. *Harry Houdini: A Magical Life.* **Tonawanda, NY: Kids Can Press, 2005.** Text, photos, movie stills, and posters depict Harry Houdini's life and work.

WEBSITES

AKA Houdini
http://www.akahoudini.org/htdocs/index.php
The Outagamie County Historical Society's History Museum in Appleton, Wisconsin, has a Harry Houdini exhibit. The website includes information about Harry's life.

The American Experience: Houdini
http://www.pbs.org/wgbh/amex/houdini/index.html
This website accompanies a public television special on Harry Houdini. It features a timeline, photographs, film clips, and secrets of Harry's escapes.

Harry Houdini

http://www.houdinitribute.com

This tribute website has a wealth of photographs, film clips, and trivia. It even includes audio clips of Harry speaking.

SELECT BIBLIOGRAPHY

Brandon, Ruth. *The Life and Many Deaths of Harry Houdini.* New York: Random House, 1993.

Christopher, Milbourne. *Houdini: A Pictorial Biography, Including More Than 250 Illustrations.* New York: Gramercy Books, 1976.

Christopher, Milbourne. *Houdini: The Untold Story.* New York: Thomas Cromwell Company, 1969.

Fleischman, Sid. *Escape! The Story of the Great Houdini.* New York: Greenwillow Books, 2006.

Gibson, Walter B. *Houdini's Escapes and Magic.* New York: Funk and Wagnalls, 1976.

Henning, Doug. *Houdini: His Legend and His Magic.* New York: Times Books, 1977.

Houdini, Harry. *A Magician Among the Spirits.* Amsterdam: Fredonia Books, 2002.

Kalush, William, and Larry Sloman. *The Secret Life of Houdini: The Making of America's First Superhero.* New York: Atria Books, 2006.

Silverman, Kenneth. *Houdini!!!: The Career of Ehrich Weiss.* New York: HarperCollins Publishers, 1996.

INDEX

Acknowledgments

The images in this book are used with the permission of: Library of Congress,
pp. 4 (LC-USZ62-112443), 8, 9 (LC-USZ62-35877), 11 (LC-USZ62-79474),
13 (LC-USZ62-112439), 15 (LC-USZC4-6048), 16 (LC-USZC2-1505),
18 (LC-USZ62-112416), 19 (LC-USZC4-3277), 23 (LC-USZC4-3293), 25
(LC-USZ62-26515), 29 (LC-USZ62-112410), 30 (LC-USZ62-112434), 33
(LC-USZ62-112421), 41, 42 (LC-USZ62-112441), 45 (right: LC-USZC4-3282);
Historic Collection/Milwaukee Public Library, p. 7; © The New York Public
Library/Art Resource, NY, pp. 14, 20; © Todd Strand/Independent Picture
Service, pp. 22 (both); The Granger Collection, New York, pp. 26, 31; AP Photo,
p. 27; © Mary Evans Picture Library/The Image Works, pp. 36, 37, 38; The
History Museum at the Castle, Appleton, WI, #2003.21.1, p. 39; © Toronto Star/
ZUMA Press, p. 40; AP Photo/Ray Stubblebine, p. 43; © Popperphoto/Getty
Images, p. 45 (left).

Front cover: Library of Congress (LC-USZ62-112420).
Back cover: Library of Congress (LC-USZC4-3290).

For quoted material: p. 5, Milbourne Christopher, *Houdini: A Pictorial Biography,
Including More Than 250 Illustrations.* (New York: Gramercy Books, 1976); pp. 5,
33, Doug Henning, *Houdini: His Legend and His Magic* (New York: Times Books,
1977).